RACHEL

No Fear

choosing faith when I am afraid

BIBLE READING PLAN & JOURNAL

No Fear
Bible Reading Plan and Journal
PUBLISHED BY RACHEL WOJO
Copyright © 2017 by Rachel Wojnarowski

Visit **www.rachelwojo.com/shop**

Requests for information should be addressed to rachel@rachelwojo.com

Trade Paperback

ISBN978-0692957936 (Rachel Wojo LLC)

ISBN-10: 0692957936

Cover design by Rachel Wojnarowski

Photo credit: Bigstock.com

Library of Congress Cataloging-in-Publication Data

Printed in the United States of America
2017—First Edition--1001

Table of Contents

Table of Contents

A Personal Note from Rachel

Dear Friend,

Thank you for beginning this wonderful journaling experience through God's Word. My goal through Bible reading is to draw closer to Jesus, and I want that for you too!

Through reading daily Bible passages, praying, and listening to God, we're going to nurture and grow our relationship with him. This Bible reading plan and journal is specifically focused on choosing faith over fear and growing faith in the roots of God's perfect love.

Our world can be an extremely fearful place when we fail to rely on God for everything. Fear can grip us so tightly that we fail to remember God's grip on us is even tighter. This Bible reading plan will help us choose to believe God's love casts out every fear we could ever have.

I'm thrilled to have you joining me! I pray you find the journaling section to be the perfect space for your individual needs.

Rachel

Choosing Faith over Fear

Welcome to the No Fear Bible Reading Plan and Journal. I'm so excited to begin this journey with you! For the next thirty-one days, we are going to dig into God's word and grow closer to Him. Together we'll decide to believe that of the over 100 times in the Bible that God said not to fear or be afraid, guess what? He meant every single one of them.

> Trusting God means you believe God is who he says he is and that he will do what he says he will do.
> --*One More Step*

Are you ready to allow the roots of your faith to grow deep into love so that your faith is BIGGER than your fear? You can share what you are learning on social media by using the hashtags #nofearjournal and #biblereadingplan. Or you can just keep it between you and God.

4 Simple Steps
to growing in faith

step 1:

Pray: Spend some time with God in prayer. Prayer is simply having a conversation with him.

step 2:

Read the Bible passage for the day one time slowly, soaking in each phrase. Read again if time allows.

step 3:

Answer the daily question.

step 4:

Complete the journaling section.

Take Heart

And about the fourth watch of the night he came to them, walking on the sea. He meant to pass by them, but when they saw him walking on the sea they thought it was a ghost, and cried out, for they all saw him and were terrified. But immediately he spoke to them and said, "Take heart; it is I. Do not be afraid." And he got into the boat with them, and the wind ceased. And they were utterly astounded, for they did not understand about the loaves, but their hearts were hardened. Mark 6:48-52

They spent every day and night with Jesus- these disciples he had called to work for the kingdom. After witnessing the miracle of Jesus feeding the five thousand with a little bread and fish, Jesus sent them ahead while he dismissed the crowd. He needed time to be alone and pray.

Mark, the gospel writer, explains that Jesus was praying alone on land while the disciples went out to sea. As the disciples strained against the oars due to the wind, Jesus began walking on the sea out towards them. But just as he was walking by their boat, they saw him and were terrified because they thought Jesus was a ghost. There are a lot of things that he could have said at this moment. But what did Jesus immediately say to his disciples?

"Take heart! It is I. Don't be afraid."

I need the reminder from the Master often. To remember that the One who created the sea controls it. To remember that the One who walks on water holds my hand. To remember that there is no need to fear because perfect love casts out all fear.

John 14:23-31   *Day 1*

Heart

Press into the promise.
Which verse speaks
loudest to my heart?

_____
_____
_____
_____
_____
_____
_____
_____

I want to rest
in the love of Jesus.

Today I will focus on feeding my faith and starving my fear through one or more of the following ideas:
(Circle your focus.)

Reviewing the promise that I listed above.

Remembering God provides courage to face my fears.

Praying for strength to fight fear in the moment.

Realizing God is with me and I don't need to be afraid.

Write out a fear that prevents your faith from growing. How can you apply today's passage to your specific fear?

_____

_____

_____

_____

_____

_____

_____

Pen A Prayer

Tell God your fears and ask for courage to overcome.

_____

_____

_____

_____

_____

_____

_____

With

His presence
never leaves me.

Lean into the Word.
Which phrase from
the passage combats
fear?

_____
_____
_____
_____
_____
_____
_____
_____
_____
_____

Today I will focus on feeding my faith and starving my fear
through one or more of the following ideas:
(Circle your focus.)

Asking the Lord to help me be more aware of his presence.

Telling specific fears that Christ has already won the war.

Reaching for more Scripture to refute a fearful spirit.

Focusing on God's love blanketed around me.

Think of a fear you have faced or are facing. When this fear presents itself, how do you typically respond? Based on today's passage, what simple action could you take in place of your usual reaction to fear?

_____

_____

_____

_____

_____

_____

_____

_____

Pen A Prayer

Tell God your fears and ask for courage to overcome.

_____

_____

_____

_____

_____

_____

_____

1 John 4:13-21   **Day 3**

Preserves

Only the perfect
love of Christ
casts out fear.

Press into the promise.
Which verse speaks
loudest to my heart?

_____
_____
_____
_____
_____
_____
_____
_____

Today I will focus on feeding my faith and starving my
fear through one or more of the following ideas:
(Circle your focus.)

Reviewing the promise that I listed above.

Remembering God provides courage to face my fears.

Praying for strength to fight fear in the moment.

Realizing God is with me and I don't need to be afraid.

Write out a fear that prevents your faith from growing. How can you apply today's passage to your specific fear?

_____

_____

_____

_____

_____

_____

_____

_____

Pen A Prayer

Tell God your fears and ask for courage to overcome.

_____

_____

_____

_____

_____

_____

_____

_____

The battle

is the

Lord's.

I Samuel 17:47

Choice

I can choose
faith over fear.

Lean into the Word.
Which phrase from
the passage combats
fear?

_____
_____
_____
_____
_____
_____
_____
_____
_____

**Today I will focus on feeding my faith and starving my fear
through one or more of the following ideas:**
(Circle your focus.)

Asking the Lord to help me be more aware of his presence.

Telling specific fears that Christ has already won the war.

Reaching for more Scripture to refute a fearful spirit.

Focusing on God's love blanketed around me.

Think of a fear you have faced or are facing. When this fear presents itself, how do you typically respond? Based on today's passage, what simple action could you take in place of your usual reaction to fear?

_____

_____

_____

_____

_____

_____

_____

Pen A Prayer

Tell God your fears and ask for courage to overcome.

_____

_____

_____

_____

_____

_____

_____

Fear Not

He knows
my name.

Press into the promise.
Which verse speaks
loudest to my heart?

_____
_____
_____
_____
_____
_____
_____
_____

**Today I will focus on feeding my faith and starving my
fear through one or more of the following ideas:**
(Circle your focus.)

Reviewing the promise that I listed above.

Remembering God provides courage to face my fears.

Praying for strength to fight fear in the moment.

Realizing God is with me and I don't need to be afraid.

Write out a fear that prevents your faith from growing. How can you apply today's passage to your specific fear?

_____

_____

_____

_____

_____

_____

_____

Pen A Prayer

Tell God your fears and ask for courage to overcome.

_____

_____

_____

_____

_____

_____

_____

Seek

If fear is comfortable, then my faith must be distant.

Lean into the Word. Which phrase from the passage combats fear?

_____
_____
_____
_____
_____
_____
_____
_____

Today I will focus on feeding my faith and starving my fear through one or more of the following ideas:
(Circle your focus.)

Asking the Lord to help me be more aware of his presence.

Telling specific fears that Christ has already won the war.

Reaching for more Scripture to refute a fearful spirit.

Focusing on God's love blanketed around me.

Think of a fear you have faced or are facing. When this fear presents itself, how do you typically respond? Based on today's passage, what simple action could you take in place of your usual reaction to fear?

_____

_____

_____

_____

_____

_____

_____

_____

Pen A Prayer

Tell God your fears and ask for courage to overcome.

_____

_____

_____

_____

_____

_____

_____

When things
seem
out of control,
God is
always
in control.

—Rachel Wojo,
One More Step

Near

The Lord my God
goes with me.

Press into the promise.
Which verse speaks
loudest to my heart?
_____
_____
_____
_____
_____
_____
_____
_____

**Today I will focus on feeding my faith and starving my
fear through one or more of the following ideas:**
(Circle your focus.)

Reviewing the promise that I listed above.

Remembering God provides courage to face my fears.

Praying for strength to fight fear in the moment.

Realizing God is with me and I don't need to be afraid.

Write out a fear that prevents your faith from growing. How can you apply today's passage to your specific fear?

_____

_____

_____

_____

_____

_____

_____

Pen A Prayer

Tell God your fears and ask for courage to overcome.

_____

_____

_____

_____

_____

_____

_____

Strong

He will not
forsake you.

Lean into the Word.
Which phrase from
the passage combats
fear?

_____
_____
_____
_____
_____
_____
_____
_____
_____

**Today I will focus on feeding my faith and starving my fear
through one or more of the following ideas:**
(Circle your focus.)

Asking the Lord to help me be more aware of his presence.

Telling specific fears that Christ has already won the war.

Reaching for more Scripture to refute a fearful spirit.

Focusing on God's love blanketed around me.

Think of a fear you have faced or are facing. When this fear presents itself, how do you typically respond? Based on today's passage, what simple action could you take in place of your usual reaction to fear?

_____

_____

_____

_____

_____

_____

_____

_____

Pen A Prayer

Tell God your fears and ask for courage to overcome.

_____

_____

_____

_____

_____

_____

_____

Hebrews 13:1-8

Assured

There is no reason
to be afraid.

Press into the promise.
Which verse speaks
loudest to my heart?

_____
_____
_____
_____
_____
_____
_____
_____

**Today I will focus on feeding my faith and starving my
fear through one or more of the following ideas:**
(Circle your focus.)

Reviewing the promise that I listed above.

Remembering God provides courage to face my fears.

Praying for strength to fight fear in the moment.

Realizing God is with me and I don't need to be afraid.

Write out a fear that prevents your faith from growing. How can you apply today's passage to your specific fear?

_____

_____

_____

_____

_____

_____

_____

Pen A Prayer

Tell God your fears and ask for courage to overcome.

_____

_____

_____

_____

_____

_____

_____

Feed your fears
and your faith will starve.
Feed your faith,
and your fears will.
Max Lucado, Fearless

Firm

Trusting means
leaving
the "what if's?"
in God's hands.

*Lean into the Word.
Which phrase from
the passage combats
fear?*

_____
_____
_____
_____
_____
_____
_____
_____

**Today I will focus on feeding my faith and starving my fear
through one or more of the following ideas:**
(Circle your focus.)

Asking the Lord to help me be more aware of his presence.

Telling specific fears that Christ has already won the war.

Reaching for more Scripture to refute a fearful spirit.

Focusing on God's love blanketed around me.

Think of a fear you have faced or are facing. When this fear presents itself, how do you typically respond? Based on today's passage, what simple action could you take in place of your usual reaction to fear?

_____

_____

_____

_____

_____

_____

_____

Pen A Prayer

Tell God your fears and ask for courage to overcome.

_____

_____

_____

_____

_____

_____

_____

Be strong,

And courageous.

And do it.

1 Chronicles 28:20

Trust

*Press into the promise.
Which verse speaks
loudest to my heart?*

I will not be
afraid; God is
my strength.

_____
_____
_____
_____
_____
_____
_____

**Today I will focus on feeding my faith and starving my
fear through one or more of the following ideas:**
(Circle your focus.)

Reviewing the promise that I listed above.

Remembering God provides courage to face my fears.

Praying for strength to fight fear in the moment.

Realizing God is with me and I don't need to be afraid.

Write out a fear that prevents your faith from growing. How can you apply today's passage to your specific fear?

_____

_____

_____

_____

_____

_____

_____

_____

Pen A Prayer

Tell God your fears and ask for courage to overcome.

_____

_____

_____

_____

_____

_____

_____

Safe

The One who created my hands promises to steady them.

Lean into the Word. Which phrase from the passage combats fear?

_____
_____
_____
_____
_____
_____
_____
_____
_____

Today I will focus on feeding my faith and starving my fear through one or more of the following ideas:
(Circle your focus.)

Asking the Lord to help me be more aware of his presence.

Telling specific fears that Christ has already won the war.

Reaching for more Scripture to refute a fearful spirit.

Focusing on God's love blanketed around me.

Think of a fear you have faced or are facing. When this fear presents itself, how do you typically respond? Based on today's passage, what simple action could you take in place of your usual reaction to fear?

_____

_____

_____

_____

_____

_____

_____

_____

Pen A Prayer

Tell God your fears and ask for courage to overcome.

_____

_____

_____

_____

_____

_____

_____

Delight

The battle is
God's.

Press into the promise.
Which verse speaks
loudest to my heart?

_____
_____
_____
_____
_____
_____
_____
_____
_____

**Today I will focus on feeding my faith and starving my
fear through one or more of the following ideas:**
(Circle your focus.)

Reviewing the promise that I listed above.

Remembering God provides courage to face my fears.

Praying for strength to fight fear in the moment.

Realizing God is with me and I don't need to be afraid.

Write out a fear that prevents your faith from growing. How can you apply today's passage to your specific fear?

_____

_____

_____

_____

_____

_____

_____

_____

.

Pen A Prayer

Tell God your fears and ask for courage to overcome.

_____

_____

_____

_____

_____

_____

_____

Fear not, I am with thee;
O be not dismayed,
for I am thy God
and will still give thee aid.
I'll strengthen thee,
help thee,
and cause thee to stand,
upheld by My righteous,
omnipotent hand.

— *George Keith*
How Firm a Foundation

Center

If I center on Jesus,
everything I say
and do will be
grounded.

Lean into the Word.
Which phrase from
the passage combats
fear?

_____
_____
_____
_____
_____
_____
_____
_____

Today I will focus on feeding my faith and starving my fear through one or more of the following ideas:
(Circle your focus.)

Asking the Lord to help me be more aware of his presence.

Telling specific fears that Christ has already won the war.

Reaching for more Scripture to refute a fearful spirit.

Focusing on God's love blanketed around me.

Think of a fear you have faced or are facing. When this fear presents itself, how do you typically respond? Based on today's passage, what simple action could you take in place of your usual reaction to fear?

_____

_____

_____

_____

_____

_____

_____

Pen A Prayer

Tell God your fears and ask for courage to overcome.

_____

_____

_____

_____

_____

_____

_____

_____

Promised

My battle plan is
orchestrated by
the ultimate
victor, Jesus.

*Press into the promise.
Which verse speaks
loudest to my heart?*

_____
_____
_____
_____
_____
_____
_____
_____
_____

**Today I will focus on feeding my faith and starving my
fear through one or more of the following ideas:**
(Circle your focus.)

Reviewing the promise that I listed above.

Remembering God provides courage to face my fears.

Praying for strength to fight fear in the moment.

Realizing God is with me and I don't need to be afraid.

Write out a fear that prevents your faith from growing. How can you apply today's passage to your specific fear?

_____

_____

_____

_____

_____

_____

_____

_____

Pen A Prayer

Tell God your fears and ask for courage to overcome.

_____

_____

_____

_____

_____

_____

_____

_____

True

God has never changed.

Lean into the Word.
Which phrase from
the passage combats
fear?

_____
_____
_____
_____
_____
_____
_____
_____
_____

Today I will focus on feeding my faith and starving my fear through one or more of the following ideas:
(Circle your focus.)

Asking the Lord to help me be more aware of his presence.

Telling specific fears that Christ has already won the war.

Reaching for more Scripture to refute a fearful spirit.

Focusing on God's love blanketed around me.

Think of a fear you have faced or are facing. When this fear presents itself, how do you typically respond? Based on today's passage, what simple action could you take in place of your usual reaction to fear?

_____

_____

_____

_____

_____

_____

_____

Pen A Prayer

Tell God your fears and ask for courage to overcome.

_____

_____

_____

_____

_____

_____

_____

How very little

can be done

under a spirit of fear.

—Florence Nightingale

Remember

Press into the promise.
Which verse speaks
loudest to my heart?

_____
_____
There is no one   _____
like God.   _____
                        _____
                        _____
                        _____
                        _____
                        _____
                        _____

Today I will focus on feeding my faith and starving my fear through one or more of the following ideas:
(Circle your focus.)

Reviewing the promise that I listed above.

Remembering God provides courage to face my fears.

Praying for strength to fight fear in the moment.

Realizing God is with me and I don't need to be afraid.

Write out a fear that prevents your faith from growing. How can you apply today's passage to your specific fear?

_____

_____

_____

_____

_____

_____

_____

_____

Pen A Prayer

Tell God your fears and ask for courage to overcome.

_____

_____

_____

_____

_____

_____

_____

Depth

God's faithfulness
supersedes fear
no matter the
time or season.

Lean into the Word.
Which phrase from
the passage combats
fear?

_____
_____
_____
_____
_____
_____
_____
_____

**Today I will focus on feeding my faith and starving my fear
through one or more of the following ideas:**
(Circle your focus.)

Asking the Lord to help me be more aware of his presence.

Telling specific fears that Christ has already won the war.

Reaching for more Scripture to refute a fearful spirit.

Focusing on God's love blanketed around me.

Think of a fear you have faced or are facing. When this fear presents itself, how do you typically respond? Based on today's passage, what simple action could you take in place of your usual reaction to fear?

_____

_____

_____

_____

_____

_____

_____

_____

Pen A Prayer

Tell God your fears and ask for courage to overcome.

_____

_____

_____

_____

_____

_____

_____

_____

Guard

Thank-you, Lord,
for sending help
before I even know
I need it.

*Press into the promise.
Which verse speaks
loudest to my heart?*

_____
_____
_____
_____
_____
_____
_____
_____

Today I will focus on feeding my faith and starving my fear through one or more of the following ideas:
(Circle your focus.)

Reviewing the promise that I listed above.

Remembering God provides courage to face my fears.

Praying for strength to fight fear in the moment.

Realizing God is with me and I don't need to be afraid.

Write out a fear that prevents your faith from growing. How can you apply today's passage to your specific fear?

_____

_____

_____

_____

_____

_____

_____

_____

Pen A Prayer

Tell God your fears and ask for courage to overcome.

_____

_____

_____

_____

_____

_____

_____

_____

Strong

No matter what
grabs at my heart,
God's grip on me
is tighter.

Lean into the Word.
Which phrase from
the passage combats
fear?

_____
_____
_____
_____
_____
_____
_____
_____

**Today I will focus on feeding my faith and starving my fear
through one or more of the following ideas:**
(Circle your focus.)

Asking the Lord to help me be more aware of his presence.

Telling specific fears that Christ has already won the war.

Reaching for more Scripture to refute a fearful spirit.

Focusing on God's love blanketed around me.

Think of a fear you have faced or are facing. When this fear presents itself, how do you typically respond? Based on today's passage, what simple action could you take in place of your usual reaction to fear?

_____

_____

_____

_____

_____

_____

_____

Pen A Prayer

Tell God your fears and ask for courage to overcome.

_____

_____

_____

_____

_____

_____

_____

Fruitful

Press into the promise.
Which verse speaks
loudest to my heart?

_____
_____
_____
_____
_____
_____
_____
_____

Fear, guilt and
shame belong in
the past.

**Today I will focus on feeding my faith and starving my
fear through one or more of the following ideas:**
(Circle your focus.)

Reviewing the promise that I listed above.

Remembering God provides courage to face my fears.

Praying for strength to fight fear in the moment.

Realizing God is with me and I don't need to be afraid.

Write out a fear that prevents your faith from growing. How can you apply today's passage to your specific fear?

_____

_____

_____

_____

_____

_____

_____

_____

.

Pen A Prayer

Tell God your fears and ask for courage to overcome.

_____

_____

_____

_____

_____

_____

_____

*Fear arises
when we imagine
that everything
depends on us.*

–Elizabeth Elliott

Life

Say goodbye to
fear and hello to
powerful living
through Christ.

Lean into the Word.
Which phrase from
the passage combats
fear?

_____
_____
_____
_____
_____
_____
_____
_____
_____

**Today I will focus on feeding my faith and starving my fear
through one or more of the following ideas:**
(Circle your focus.)

Asking the Lord to help me be more aware of his presence.

Telling specific fears that Christ has already won the war.

Reaching for more Scripture to refute a fearful spirit.

Focusing on God's love blanketed around me.

Think of a fear you have faced or are facing. When this fear presents itself, how do you typically respond? Based on today's passage, what simple action could you take in place of your usual reaction to fear?

_____

_____

_____

_____

_____

_____

_____

_____

Pen A Prayer

Tell God your fears and ask for courage to overcome.

_____

_____

_____

_____

_____

_____

_____

Offer

The power of
God enables me
to stand with
no fear.

Press into the promise.
Which verse speaks
loudest to my heart?

_____
_____
_____
_____
_____
_____
_____
_____

**Today I will focus on feeding my faith and starving my
fear through one or more of the following ideas:**
(Circle your focus.)

Reviewing the promise that I listed above.

Remembering God provides courage to face my fears.

Praying for strength to fight fear in the moment.

Realizing God is with me and I don't need to be afraid.

Write out a fear that prevents your faith from growing. How can you apply today's passage to your specific fear?

_____

_____

_____

_____

_____

_____

_____

_____

Pen A Prayer

Tell God your fears and ask for courage to overcome.

_____

_____

_____

_____

_____

_____

_____

_____

Be strong
in the Lord
and his
mighty power.
Ephesians 4:10

Psalm 3:1-8   Day 24

Support

Lean into the Word.
Which phrase from
the passage combats
fear?

_____
_____
_____

God is always
at my aid.

_____
_____
_____
_____
_____
_____
_____

**Today I will focus on feeding my faith and starving my fear
through one or more of the following ideas:**
(Circle your focus.)

Asking the Lord to help me be more aware of his presence.

Telling specific fears that Christ has already won the war.

Reaching for more Scripture to refute a fearful spirit.

Focusing on God's love blanketed around me.

Think of a fear you have faced or are facing. When this fear presents itself, how do you typically respond? Based on today's passage, what simple action could you take in place of your usual reaction to fear?

_____

_____

_____

_____

_____

_____

_____

_____

Pen A Prayer

Tell God your fears and ask for courage to overcome.

_____

_____

_____

_____

_____

_____

_____

Psalm 27:1-5

Fortress

Press into the promise.
Which verse speaks
loudest to my heart?

_____
_____
_____
_____
_____
_____
_____
_____

Fight
worry and fear
with worship and
faith.

Today I will focus on feeding my faith and starving my fear through one or more of the following ideas:
(Circle your focus.)

Reviewing the promise that I listed above.

Remembering God provides courage to face my fears.

Praying for strength to fight fear in the moment.

Realizing God is with me and I don't need to be afraid.

Write out a fear that prevents your faith from growing. How can you apply today's passage to your specific fear?

_____

_____

_____

_____

_____

_____

_____

_____

Pen A Prayer

Tell God your fears and ask for courage to overcome.

_____

_____

_____

_____

_____

_____

_____

Faith does not
eliminate questions.
But faith knows
where to take them.

Elizabeth Elliott

Meditate

Remember what God has done in the past.

Lean into the Word.
Which phrase from the passage combats fear?

_____
_____
_____
_____
_____
_____
_____
_____
_____

Today I will focus on feeding my faith and starving my fear through one or more of the following ideas:
(Circle your focus.)

Asking the Lord to help me be more aware of his presence.

Telling specific fears that Christ has already won the war.

Reaching for more Scripture to refute a fearful spirit.

Focusing on God's love blanketed around me.

Think of a fear you have faced or are facing. When this fear presents itself, how do you typically respond? Based on today's passage, what simple action could you take in place of your usual reaction to fear?

_____

_____

_____

_____

_____

_____

_____

Pen A Prayer

Tell God your fears and ask for courage to overcome.

_____

_____

_____

_____

_____

_____

_____

Level

God's
righteousness
brings my soul out
of trouble.

Press into the promise.
Which verse speaks
loudest to my heart?

_____
_____
_____
_____
_____
_____
_____
_____
_____

Today I will focus on feeding my faith and starving my fear
through one or more of the following ideas:
(Circle your focus.)

Reviewing the promise that I listed above.

Remembering God provides courage to face my fears.

Praying for strength to fight fear in the moment.

Realizing God is with me and I don't need to be afraid.

Write out a fear that prevents your faith from growing. How can you apply today's passage to your specific fear?

_____

_____

_____

_____

_____

_____

_____

Pen A Prayer

Tell God your fears and ask for courage to overcome.

_____

_____

_____

_____

_____

_____

_____

Not Afraid

God is
with me.

*Lean into the Word.
Which phrase from
the passage combats
fear?*

_____
_____
_____
_____
_____
_____
_____
_____
_____

**Today I will focus on feeding my faith and starving my fear
through one or more of the following ideas:**
(Circle your focus.)

Asking the Lord to help me be more aware of his presence.

Telling specific fears that Christ has already won the war.

Reaching for more Scripture to refute a fearful spirit.

Focusing on God's love blanketed around me.

Think of a fear you have faced or are facing. When this fear presents itself, how do you typically respond? Based on today's passage, what simple action could you take in place of your usual reaction to fear?

_____

_____

_____

_____

_____

_____

_____

_____

Pen A Prayer

Tell God your fears and ask for courage to overcome.

_____

_____

_____

_____

_____

_____

_____

Infectious

Fear is contagious.
And so is courage.

*Press into the promise.
Which verse speaks
loudest to my heart?*

_____
_____
_____
_____
_____
_____
_____
_____
_____

Today I will focus on feeding my faith and starving my fear through one or more of the following ideas:
(Circle your focus.)

Reviewing the promise that I listed above.

Remembering God provides courage to face my fears.

Praying for strength to fight fear in the moment.

Realizing God is with me and I don't need to be afraid.

Write out a fear that prevents your faith from growing. How can you apply today's passage to your specific fear?

_____

_____

_____

_____

_____

_____

_____

Pen A Prayer

Tell God your fears and ask for courage to overcome.

_____

_____

_____

_____

_____

_____

_____

Jeremiah 17:5-10   *Day 30*

Planted

Lean into the Word.
Which phrase from
the passage combats
fear?

I am growing in
Christ. There is
no reason to fear.

_____
_____
_____
_____
_____
_____
_____
_____
_____

**Today I will focus on feeding my faith and starving my fear
through one or more of the following ideas:**
(Circle your focus.)

Asking the Lord to help me be more aware of his presence.

Telling specific fears that Christ has already won the war.

Reaching for more Scripture to refute a fearful spirit.

Focusing on God's love blanketed around me.

Think of a fear you have faced or are facing. When this fear presents itself, how do you typically respond? Based on today's passage, what simple action could you take in place of your usual reaction to fear?

_____

_____

_____

_____

_____

_____

_____

Pen A Prayer

Tell God your fears and ask for courage to overcome.

_____

_____

_____

_____

_____

_____

_____

Ever-Present

Press into the promise.
Which verse speaks
loudest to my heart?

_____
_____
Man cannot harm
_____
what God
_____
protects.
_____
_____
_____
_____

**Today I will focus on feeding my faith and starving my
fear through one or more of the following ideas:**
(Circle your focus.)

Reviewing the promise that I listed above.

Remembering God provides courage to face my fears.

Praying for strength to fight fear in the moment.

Realizing God is with me and I don't need to be afraid.

Write out a fear that prevents your faith from growing. How can you apply today's passage to your specific fear?

_____

_____

_____

_____

_____

_____

_____

_____

.

Pen A Prayer

Tell God your fears and ask for courage to overcome.

_____

_____

_____

_____

_____

_____

_____

Put a Bow on It!

You did it! You read your Bible for 31 days in a row!

Throughout this month of Scripture reading, I've been reminded anew that my source of strength and courage must be the Lord. When fear tries to strike me down or panic threatens me, God's Word restores my soul.

I pray that as you've walked this 31-day path, you've enjoyed the journaling methods and each exercise has provided methods of not only coping with fear, but overcoming it!

I hope you'll you continue to let your faith grow bigger than your fear!

Thanks for joining me on this journey through the Bible. Discover more Bible reading plans & journals at rachelwojo.com/shop.

Additional Notes

About the Author

Rachel "Wojo" Wojnarowski is wife to Matt and mom to seven wonderful kids. Her greatest passion is inspiring others to welcome Jesus into their lives and enjoy the abundant life he offers.

As a sought-after blogger and writer, she sees thousands of readers visit her blog daily. Rachel leads community ladies' Bible studies in central Ohio and serves as an event planner and speaker. In her "free time" she crochets, knits, and sews handmade clothing. Okay, not really. She enjoys running and she's a tech geek at heart.

Reader, writer, speaker, and dreamer, Rachel can be found on her website at **www.RachelWojo.com**.

Free Bible Study Video Series

If you enjoyed this Bible reading plan & journal, then you'll love Rachel's free video Bible study to help you find strength for difficult seasons of life! **http://rachelwojo.com/free-bible-study-video-series-for-one-more-step/**

Feel like giving up?

Are you ready to quit? Give up? But deep down, you want to figure out how to keep on keeping on?

Like you, Rachel has faced experiences that crushed her dreams of the perfect life: a failed marriage, a daughter's heartbreaking diagnosis, and more. In this book, she transparently shares her pain and empathizes with yours, then points you to the path of God's Word, where you'll find hope to carry you forward. One More Step gives you permission to ache freely—and helps you believe that life won't always be this hard. No matter the circumstances you face, through these pages you'll learn to...

- persevere through out-of-control circumstances and gain a more intimate relationship with Jesus
- run to God's Word when discouragement strikes
- replace feelings of despair with truths of Scripture

BUY NOW
www.rachelwojo.com/onemorestep

If you enjoyed this Bible reading plan and journal, then you'll love:

RACHEL WOJO

Pure Joy

cultivating a
happy heart

BIBLE READING PLAN & JOURNAL

RACHEL WOJO

True Love

embracing the Father's affection

BIBLE READING PLAN & JOURNAL

RACHEL WOJO

Perfect Peace

planting my eyes on Jesus

BIBLE READING PLAN & JOURNAL

RACHEL WOJO

Confident Trust

believing God's plan is best

BIBLE READING PLAN & JOURNAL

RACHEL WOJO

Never Alone

remembering
God is with me

BIBLE READING PLAN & JOURNAL

RACHEL WOJO

Soul Secure

winning over worry
through God's Word

BIBLE READING PLAN & JOURNAL

RACHEL WOJO

Purposeful Pause

waiting on God's perfect timing

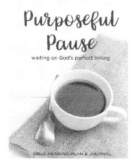

BIBLE READING PLAN & JOURNAL

RACHEL WOJO

Everything Beautiful

savoring God's seasonal elegance

BIBLE READING PLAN & JOURNAL

RACHEL WOJO

Magnificent Power

recognizing God is bigger than anything

BIBLE READING PLAN & JOURNAL

Made in the USA
Middletown, DE
01 July 2019